LIFE IN ABUNDANCE

THE CAFOD/ CHRISTIAN AID
LENT BOOK 2009

David Adam   •   John Bell
Joseph Donders   •   Shirley du Boulay
Jon Sweeney   •   Frances Young

LIFE IN ABUNDANCE

Reflections on the
Scripture Readings for Lent 2009

First published in Great Britain in 2008 by

CAFOD
Romero Close
Stockwell Road
London SW9 9TY

Christian Aid
35 Lower Marsh
London SE1 7RL

Darton, Longman and Todd Ltd
1 Spencer Court
140-142 Wandsworth High Street
London SW18 4JJ

ISBN 0 232 52754 7

Bible quotations are taken predominantly from the New Jerusalem
Bible, published and copyright © 1985 by Darton, Longman and Todd
Ltd and Doubleday, a division of Random House, Inc.

Note: the Hebrew numbering of the Psalms is used. From Psalm 10 to
147 this is ahead of the Greek and Vulgate numbering which is used
in some psalters.

Text designed and produced by Sandie Boccacci
Set in 9.5/13pt Palatino
Printed and bound in Great Britain by
Athenaeum Press Ltd, Gateshead, Tyne and Wear

Contents

Joseph G. Donders, a member of the Missionaries of Africa, is Professor Emeritus in Mission and Cross-cultural Studies at the Washington Theological Union, in Washington DC. He has lectured all over the world and is the author of several books.

Jon M. Sweeney, a writer, editor, and retreat leader, is the associate publisher at Paraclete Press in Massachusetts. and lives in Vermont, USA. His books include *Light in the Dark Ages: The Friendship of Francis and Clare of Assisi*.

John L. Bell is an ordained minister of the Church of Scotland and a Member of the Iona Community, and its Wild Goose Resource Group. He is a hymnwriter, author and broadcaster, lecturing and preaching across the denominations in Europe, North America and Australasia, but is primarily concerned with the renewal of congregational worship at grass roots level.

Shirley du Boulay worked at the BBC in the Music Department before becoming a producer, first in radio, then in television, where she made documentaries and films. She resigned in 1978 and since has written several books, including biographies of Desmond Tutu and Teresa of Avila.

Frances M. Young is Emeritus Professor of the University of Birmingham, and an ordained minister of the Methodist Church. The author of many books on patristics, she received the OBE in 1998 for services to Theology and is a Fellow of the British Academy. Her most recent book is *Brokenness and Blessing*.

David Adam was born in Alnwick, Northumberland. When he left school at 15, he went to work underground in the coal mines for three years. He was vicar of Danby in North Yorkshire for over 20 years, where he began writing prayers that helped to revive popular interest in the Celtic spirituality. He later became vicar of Holy Island, Lindisfarne, where he ministered to thousands of pilgrims and other visitors.

In *Life in Abundance* six writers open up the word of God to us, a word that invites us to a new way of seeing, a conversion of heart, and a renewed determination to create a just world.

During Lent we prepare for Easter, when Christians celebrate the rising from the dead of Jesus by prayer and fasting and the giving of alms to the poor. Forty days of penance. Forty days of renewal of our relationship with God.

The church's readings during the season of Lent speak of the glory of creation, and the preciousness of every human being. We are asked to love God with all our heart and with all our soul and with all our mind. And we are asked to love our neighbour as ourself.

In these Lenten readings and reflections we discover what the first things are, and we commit ourselves to do the first things first. Are love, justice, forgiveness, prayer the things that *really* matter to me? What sort of person am I – and what sort of person do I want to be? Is getting to know God is the real passion of my life? Is prayer and the search for justice at the heart of my life?

Each time we catch the eye of a person in need, each time we meet a hungry person, each time we listen to a stranger's story, we are meeting Jesus. Each time we stop for a moment and pay attention, each time we listen, each time we help, we are meeting Jesus, and the door of heaven opens for a few seconds.

In listening and watching and serving others we do not 'find God' but discover that God has been there all the time. Closer to us than the air we breathe.

Brendan Walsh

LIFE IN ABUNDANCE

THE CAFOD/ CHRISTIAN AID
LENT BOOK 2009

Joseph Donders

Ash Wednesday to Saturday after Ash Wednesday

Ash Wednesday

Let your hearts be broken!

Jl 2:12–18; Ps 51; 2 Cor 5:20–6:2; Mt 6:1–6, 16–18

> *'But now, now – it is Yahweh who speaks – come back to me with all your heart!* (Joel 2:12)

There is something universal about Ash Wednesday. Even people who hardly ever go to church during the rest of the year sometimes make the effort of receiving ashes on their forehead today.

There are so many sharing the ashes that it is not only something you do as an individual. It is a shared gesture, a common acknowledgment of who we are, 'dust and to dust shall we return', and 'sinners who intend to turn away from sin and be faithful to the gospel'. Lining up to receive those ashes on our forehead is an intriguing experience. Young and old, rich and poor, known and unknown, all are lining up in the same way to enter forty days of penance and renewal.

Clearly, this gesture should not just be an expression of wishful thinking, or, even worse, a mere show. Jesus warns us in today's gospel against this, several times using the the word 'hypocrite'. He even, rather ironically, suggests that we do not smudge our faces, but wash them, when we decide to fast. This is his way of expressing what he thought about people who considered themselves not only 'holier-than-thou' but 'holier-than-they-themselves'. Jesus warns us not to wear a pious mask without anything behind it corresponding to it.

Saint Augustine left us in one of his sermons a further warning, even if you do fast: 'Don't believe that fasting suffices. Fasting punishes you, but it does not restore your brother ... How many poor people could be nourished by the meal you did not take today?' He is referring to what the prophet Isaiah wrote centuries earlier in the name of Yahweh: 'Is not this the sort of fasting that pleases me – to share your bread with the hungry?'

The prophet Joel puts it – also in the name of Yahweh – in a different way: 'Let your hearts be broken!' And, opening our hearts, Joel suggests, be Godlike, 'full of tenderness and compassion, slow to anger, rich in graciousness, and ready to relent.'

Thought for the day:
Let me today open my heart for God's compassion and graciousness.

Prayer
Loving God,
fill me with compassion for others
especially for those in need,
let me respond
sharing in your love
for all of us.
Amen

3

Taking up his cross every day

Dt 30:15–20; Ps 1; Lk 9:22–25

> *'Let him renounce himself and take up his cross every day and follow me.'* (Luke 9:24)

When we speak about or think of Jesus' cross we almost spontaneously think about him being crucified and hanging on the cross. In the gospel reading of today Jesus himself warns his disciples of his forthcoming death on the cross.

But that is not all we should be thinking of when meditating on his cross. It could not be, because Jesus himself tells us to take up his cross *daily:* 'If anyone wants to be a follower of mine, let him renounce himself and take up his cross every day and follow me.'

This is more than a piece of advice about how we should live, that we can take or leave as we choose. More than once he warns us starkly, 'Whoever does not carry the cross and follow me cannot be my disciple' (14:27).

Jesus uses the word 'daily' when speaking about our mission, about our carrying of his cross. It is not something that should remain just a lofty ideal. It is something to be put into practice in every choice, in every decision, in all our tribulations and conflicts each day and all through the day. Taking up his cross is about justice, peace and care for the whole of creation. It is about the introduction and realisation of God's Kingdom in this world.

It means that we should say 'No' to all that tempts us not to walk our way with Jesus, not to take up his cross.

But taking up our cross is not only a question of saying 'No'. It does not mean that we should indulge in self-imposed and life-debasing mortifications for their own sake. It is at the same time a question of saying 'Yes' to accompanying Jesus 'into the way of peace' (Lk 1:79) in our world. It means that we take his way of life as our norm in the world in which we live, in all our personal and corporate deliberations and decisions.

Walking Jesus' 'Way' is an ongoing affair. In those who walk and live it, the reign of God has come 'among us'. To follow his Way, to carry his cross daily, will colour their lives from moment to moment.

Thought for the day
Recall a person, who followed Jesus' Way in an exemplary way.

Prayer
Lord Jesus,
help me realize that you are always with me
on my sometimes difficult journey through life.
Let me remember that you are beside me,
and before me and behind me
each and every day of my life.
Amen

Is that what you call fasting?

Is 58:1–9; Ps 51; Mt 9:14–15

>   *'Is not this the sort of fasting that pleases me?'*
>   (Isaiah 58: 6)

The author of the psalm today is sure of something. He knows that he is a sinner. He also knows that sacrifices are going to be of no help, neither goats nor bullocks nor any burnt offering. Those sacrifices made to God would be refused, 'returned to sender'. He also understands something else. The only thing that would be of any help is a change of heart. A humbled, contrite heart would not be rejected.

The prophet Isaiah explains what that change of heart mean. He explains the kind of fasting and repentance that would be pleasing to God. It is not a question of sackcloth and ashes, or of simply letting your head hang down like a broken reed. What really would make a difference is sharing your shelter with the homeless, your bread with the hungry, and your clothing with the naked.

But charitable handouts alone are not enough. Justice should be done. Isaiah, speaking in the name of Yahweh, does not mince God's word: 'This is the sort of fasting that pleases me, breaking unjust fetters and undoing the thongs of the yoke.'

Blessed Frederic Ozanam, the founder of the Saint Vincent de Paul Society, the charitable organisation at work all over the world, wrote one hundred and fifty years ago about the relation between justice and charity.

'The order of society is based on two virtues', he said, 'justice and charity. However, justice presupposes a lot of love already … Justice has it limits whereas charity knows none.'

This is a truth Pope Benedict XVI stressed repeatedly in his first two encyclicals, *Deus Caritas Est* and *Spe Salvi*, on charity and hope. If you love people, you want them to be treated justly. Yet, if that was all, justice might be done, but something would be missing. What counts in the end is to love and to be loved. In the final analysis, it is not only justice but love we need.

Thought for the day
Remember an instant that you were grateful for mercy shown to you.

Prayer
Have mercy on me, O God!
Let the mercy
you show to me
colour my life
and the kindness
I show to others.
Amen

Moved by him from within

Is 58:9–14; Ps 86:1–6; Lk 5:27–32

> *'And leaving everything he got up and followed him.'*
> (Luke 5:28)

When Luke tells us today the story of the tax collector, Levi, he makes it very short. Jesus said to him simply, 'Follow me.' And, moved by Jesus from within, that's what Levi did, first throwing a great farewell reception for his colleagues and friends, to which Jesus and his disciples were also invited. It caused a bit of a scandal. Some blamed Jesus afterwards for sitting at table with Levi and his shady colleagues and friends. 'Why do you eat with tax collectors and sinners?' they asked him.

Jesus' answer to that question is to look at what happened to Levi that day. Luke, a doctor, explains this in terms he was familiar with. He tells us that Jesus had 'healed' Levi.

What made Levi break with his past and follow Jesus? The question is still asked centuries later. Think of a bishop like Oscar Romero or a religious sister like Mother Teresa of Calcutta. Why did they do the things they did? Where did their inspiration, their motivation, come from?

Think of yourself, where does your inspiration and motivation to read this reflection during this period of Lent come from?

What about the thousands of networks and organizations such as Cafod and Christian Aid whose members invest their time and goodwill in voluntary work, in supporting aid and development projects overseas and in education and campaigning for change at home? Where does the energy and courage come from in all of those who actively engage – as well as they can – in the realization of God's reign in this world, in establishing the reign of justice and peace?

The answer is, from the Spirit they recognized in Jesus. It is the Spirit of Jesus active in them. It is what Luke explained later in his follow-up book to his Gospel, The Acts of the Apostles. All graciousness and kindness, all love and respect come from that affiliation to God's loving Spirit.

Levi experienced this divine dynamics when he met Jesus. Struck by it, he felt no hesitation whatsoever when Jesus told him, 'Follow me.' He welcomed the switch in his life. With Jesus as his principal guest, he threw a party to celebrate.

Thought for the day
Pay attention today, how Jesus' Spirit, too, might stir you.

Prayer
Jesus,
you have told us
to be the light of the world.
Help me to live like that,
notwithstanding the difficulties
it might cause.
Amen

Joseph Donders

First Week of Lent

First Sunday of Lent

The new age of the Holy Spirit

Gen 9:8–15; Ps 25; 1 Peter 3:18–22; Mk 1:12–15

> *'I have baptised you with water, but he will baptise you with the Holy Spirit.'* (Mark 1:8)

There was the promise of newness hanging in the air. The newness and change everyone of good will was eagerly hoping for. The rumour had spread all over the country. A prophet had appeared from the desert, a prophet called John. He preached that things were going to change, and he invited his listeners to share in that change.

He was in a way a kind of disappointment. It is what he said of himself. He could do away with the old in them, but the realization of the new would only come with someone else.

They came nevertheless. They came from all over. One day Jesus joined them. He lined up with them, he lined up with us, waiting for his turn. He – though sinless – stepped into the mud at the bottom of the river to be baptised, to be with us in our misery. He identified himself at that moment with all those who were convinced that the world needed a change, that humanity needed redemption.

Of course we know that our world is not all good and

just. All of us know and intuit that it should change. That *we* should change to redeem and save it.

Are we really willing to go to someone like John, who was preaching a new order of things? Would we really line up in front of him, risking being found in the company of Jesus, who would bring about that change? He joined us, are we prepared to follow him?

Or are we like those sick people who do not want to go to a doctor because they are afraid to hear that they will have to change their lives? Those who do not want to undergo a medical examination in case it will show us how sick we are, and what changes we must make in our lives? Is that we are afraid to follow him?

Thought for today
Why would it be good for you to line up with Jesus at the river Jordan?

Prayer
Almighty Father,
the coming of your Son among us
is a divine sign of the hope you invest in us.
Let me catch something of that hope
in my daily life.
Amen.

On his return

Lv 19:1–2, 11–18; Ps 19; Mt 25:31–46

> *'In so far as you did this to one of the least of my brothers, you did it to me.'* (Matthew 25:40)

Jesus' disciples have always been interested in his return. Once his disciples asked him 'privately': 'Tell us when will this be, and what will be the sign of your coming and of the end of the age?' (24:3).

In his answer, Jesus does speak about his return. However, he does not speak about the future when he answers. He turns their question around. He turns their query, 'When will you return?' into, 'When did *you* return?' and he turns their question, 'When will we see you?' into, 'When did I receive you?'

We do not know when Jesus will return, but we do know where we can meet him in between, in the interval between now and then.

Every time we meet a person in need, a hungry person, someone who is thirsty, a stranger, a naked, sick or imprisoned person, and help them, we meet Jesus. 'I was hungry and you gave me to eat', 'I was a refugee and you welcomed me.'

When any of these things happen in our lives, Jesus is returning. He identifies himself with those prisoners, refugees, sick, hungry, thirsty, and naked ones. Each time our encounter takes place 'the reign of God' is being re-established, and the door of heaven opens for a moment.

This might seem somewhat unreal, a mere figment of

the imagination. It is not. It is the reality. Sometimes, it might involve real courage and heroism. But it is often the simplest things: a smile, a greeting, a cup of coffee, a helping hand, a word of help to a child, a professional job performed well at a fair price.

Our works of mercy will be needed as long as we live in a world tainted by injustice and sin. Our works of mercy and our working for justice have to be balanced. Our works of mercy should not delay our working at justice; and our working at justice should not delay our works of mercy.

Thought for today
Every time I meet a person in need I meet Jesus.

Prayer
Dear Lord,
help me to see your presence
in those in need,
so that I may not overlook
your presence in myself.
Amen.

God, parent of our globalising world

Is 55: 10–11; Ps 34; Mt 6:7–15

'So you should pray like this: "Our Father" ' (Mt 6:8)

A striking aspect of Matthew's report is the frequent use Jesus makes of the name 'Father' for God. Jesus does this over thirty times. He speaks about 'My Father', 'Your Father', 'Their Father' and 'Our Father'. In contrast, Mark's gospel, according to scholars one of Matthew's sources, does this only three times.

The two writers composed their gospels for a different readership. Matthew wrote for a group of Christians who no longer lived in their Christian enclave in Jerusalem, as they had been doing for years. Because of political developments and the fall of Jerusalem they had had to leave the city and were now living in exile, surrounded by strangers, and people with all kinds of other faiths and beliefs.

This is the situation that groups of Christians are facing more and more today all over the world. Traditionally Christian societies are rapidly disappearing. Mosques and temples are being built around them while church buildings are sometimes closing. You do not need to be a prophet to foresee the danger of cultural and religious conflict. Our daily news is full of stories of violence and terrorism grounded in religious differences and tensions.

An old bible story tells us how Noah's 72 grandsons left their grandfather's homestead years after the flood, spreading all over the earth. They all walked steadily away from each other, each family having its own history and developing its own culture. Walking further and further away from each other on a globe, one day they were bound to meet again. We are living that day! The world's peoples are pushing together as never before.

It is in this new context that Matthew's insistence on God as Our Father gets a new relevance. We should be perfect as our common Father is perfect (Matthew 5:48), loving all of us, providing all of us with the rain, the sun and the food and drink we all equally need (5:45). We all share God's breath blown in all of us.

Thought for today
Jesus: 'I was a stranger and you made me welcome'
(Matthew 25:35)

Prayer
Loving God
and Father/Mother of all of us,
help me to share
in your love
for all of us.
Amen.

And God relented

Jon 3:1–10; Ps 51; Lk 11:29–32

> *'Let everyone renounce his evil behaviour and the wicked things done.'* (Jonah 3:8)

Perhaps the best known example of repentance and sackcloth and ashes in the Old Testament is the story of Jonah and the city of Nineveh. It is a story that could stand as a kind of mirror to our own situation.

There was the reluctant prophet, Jonah. He knew about the sad situation of the city of Nineveh, and how the type of life lived there was going to lead to total disaster for the people of the city.

But even when God asked him to speak out and to do something about it, to ask the city dwellers to change their ways, Jonah dodged the issue. He was afraid of the reception he might receive. Nobody likes to listen to prophets of doom. They always risk their reputation, and sometimes even their lives.

Jonah tried to escape from it all, sailing away to Tarshish, most probably a city in Spain. What happened to him, the story of his being thrown overboard by the sailors, and of the fish that swallowed him and then spat him out on Nineveh's beach, is still remembered in children's songs and games.

When Jonah finally obeyed God's command and spoke in the great city of Nineveh, his preaching was amazingly effective. Word of his message was carried to the king of Nineveh. When the news reached him, the king rose from his throne, took off his robe, put on sackcloth, and sat in ashes. The whole city followed his example, men, women, children and even the animals they owned. It was not only a change of heart in some individuals, but a renewal of the whole of the community.

Yet Jonah, instead of feeling pleased at the success of his mission, was disappointed that God had shown mercy to the former reprobates. 'When God saw what they did and how they turned from their evil ways, God had compassion and did not bring upon them the destruction he had threatened, to the chagrin of Jonah, that prophet of doom.'

God had to remind Jonah that his mercy and compassion extended to all the peoples of the earth: 'Am I not to feel sorry for Nineveh, the great city, in which there are more than hundred and twenty thousand people who cannot tell their right hand from their left, to say nothing of all the animals?'

Thought for today
Should we not change our eating pattern considering the world's plight?

Prayer
Merciful God,
I ask with all my heart
help me not to clutter my life
with things I do not need and
that would keep me from you,
and from others.
Amen.

The reciprocity of The Golden Rule

Est 4:1–3, 5:12–14; Ps 138; Mt 7:7–12

> *'So always treat others as you would like them to treat you.'* (Matthew 7:12)

The text Matthew ascribes to Jesus, 'always treat others as you would like them to treat you', is traditionally called 'The Golden Rule'. Not only Jesus endorsed it. All the great world religions endorse it. They often use it to summarize their ethical prescriptions on how we should live our lives. It is a rule that has influenced the lives of people in many different cultures.

It is, however, a piece of advice that can be misunderstood, and that sometimes is misunderstood. It leads too often to the idea that 'giving' is more important than 'receiving'. The mutuality is lost. One ends up with 'givers' who have the gold and 'receivers' who have not.

There was once a soup kitchen run by a religious group and their volunteers in one of the world's great cities. They helped poor people with a substantial breakfast every Sunday morning after their Eucharistic celebration. When those who enjoyed the excellent breakfast, asked whether they would be allowed to help with the cleaning and the washing-up they were told, 'No, we are here to help you, you should not help us.' Some of the poor stopped coming for breakfast.

Reciprocity is implied in the golden rule. Jesus understood this well. So often, when he is healing someone, he asks the person he is helping to do something himself. For example, he tells the man healed of his blindness: 'Go and wash in the pool of Siloam.' This is what he did, and then he began to see (John 9:7).

Jesus did not hesitate to ask for help from others. At one of his great picnics, he asked the crowd, 'Is there anybody here who has anything to eat?' It was a small boy, who had some bread and some fish (John 6:9). And the boy's bread and fish fed everyone! In the end, Jesus must have been glad that Simon of Cyrene helped him to carry his cross.

Thought for today

'Only because of your love, the poor will forgive you for the bread you give them.' (St. Vincent de Paul)

Prayer

My Lord,
come to my help,
save me by your hand,
for I am alone
I have no helper but you,
Amen.

(Esther's prayer)

To forgive and to be forgiven

Ez 18:21–28; Ps 130; Mt 5:20–26

> *'Go and be reconciled with your brother first.'*
> (Matthew 5:24)

When thinking of reconciliation we often think about our need to forgive others. I should forgive my brother or sister who has offended or mistreated me. There is no doubt about that.

Yet this is not what Jesus is talking about in today's reading. He is not talking about you having something against your brother or sister who wronged you. He is talking about your brother or sister who has something against you, because you wronged him or her. It is not only you who has to forgive, but it is also you who has to be forgiven. Jesus suggests that you contact that brother or sister, and ask them for their forgiveness!

The prophet Ezekiel writes about this type of forgiveness in the first reading. We have not to forgive God for anything. God did not offend us. We offended God. We need God's forgiveness. If we are sincere, upright and willing to change our lives, God will forgive us. Love will prevail.

If I admit to my brother or sister that I wronged them, the situation might become complicated. They might ask for compensation, for justice. They might even engage a lawyer and go to court. This happened in Jesus' time, and it happens nowadays – many people seem to be almost always involved in litigation of some sort. It happens so much that the normal functioning of medical and other services is sometimes made almost impossible. Jesus asks that we avoid the misery all this causes and to settle matters amicably with each other before going to court.

Blessed Frederic Ozanam thought that the fate of the world 'will be terrible if charity does not interpose, if the force of love does not dominate.'

Thought for today
Whose side are you on, in your country and in the world?

Prayer
Loving God,
you invited me
to share in your love.
Help me to do that
in all I decide to do,
and not to do.
Amen.

The reason is given!

Dt 26: 16–19; Ps 119; Mt 5: 43–48

> *'You must be therefore be perfect just as your heavenly Father is perfect.'* (Matthew 5: 48)

God forgives. He causes the sun rise on the bad as well as on the good. Jesus warns us, though, that is not the best way of putting it; he just tells us not only that we *should* share in God's love, but that we *do* share in God's love, and that we should *live* that love. The consequence of living that reality, however, remains like a miracle in our world.

It is only two years ago that on a Monday morning an enraged gunman entered a one-room Amish Christian school in Pennsylvania. In front of 25 horrified pupils, he told the teacher and the boys present to leave the classroom. He ordered the girls to stay. He then tied the legs of the ten remaining girls and told them that he was going to shoot them, because he was angry with God for taking his little daughter.

The oldest girl, 13 years old, begged the gunman to 'shoot me first and let the others go.' He refused her offer and shot all ten of them. When the police stormed the building, he shot himself.

Half of the 75 people at the murderer's funeral were parents who had just buried their own children. They had already given their words of forgiveness to the widow of the murderer. Their forgiveness went even further than just words. They supported a fund to assist the gunman's family.

Within three weeks, the news of this Amish forgiveness had appeared in 2,900 news stories worldwide, from the *Khaleej Times* of the United Arab Emirates to Australian Television, and on at least half a million websites. Everyone wondered about this forgiveness. How could those parents do this?

Their answer was simple, though it is not a simple answer. In their response, they referred not only to the gospel text we have as our reflection today. They also referred to the reality of their sharing in the love of God, Father of all of us.

Thought for today
Grant pardon and you will be pardoned. (Luke 6:37)

Prayer
Our Father,
who art in heaven,
help us to forgive others
as you forgive them.
We ask you this
through Jesus Christ.
Amen

Jon Sweeney

Second Week of Lent

Second Sunday of Lent

What does resurrection mean?

Gen 22:1–2, 9–13, 15–18; Ps 116; Rom 8:31–4; Mk 9:2–10

> *'They observed the warning faithfully, though among themselves they discussed what "rising from the dead" could mean.'* (Mark 9:10)

I once said to a rabbi friend over dinner that I thought the Binding of Isaac – the story of Abraham attempting to sacrifice his son in Genesis chapter 22 – should have been stricken from the Torah a millennia ago. He thought I was joking, but I wasn't. If you are at all like me, the story of God putting Abraham to such a test can feel, shall I say, repulsive? Would my God do such a thing? Should we revere a man because he actually almost did it?

The traditional understanding of our passage from Genesis 22 is that we must not hold back anything from God. Everything we have, is God's and not our own. But when, if ever, have I actually believed that, let alone acted upon it? I can tell you with absolute certainty that I would never listen to a Voice that told me to sacrifice my only son. So, what, then?

Perhaps it helps to read Genesis 22 from the perspective of young Isaac, rather than from that of old Abraham. I may not be able to understand the Binding of Isaac as a father, but perhaps I can, as a needy son. It was

Isaac's actions on that fateful day that changed the course of history. Isaac, not Abraham, was ultimately faithful and sacrificial. It was Isaac who becomes the symbol of our Lord himself.

The epistle reading from St. Paul's teaching in Romans 8 becomes clearer from the perspective of Isaac, as well: Abraham is the symbol of God the Father who gave up his only Son, for us all. But it is that Son, Jesus, who gave himself up as a sacrifice for sinners, and rose again so that he might intercede on our behalf. We are dead until we rise again with him.

Thought for the day

Is there some aspect of your faith that needs resurrecting today?

Prayer

God of mercy and love,
you are our only God,
the only One – who
can truly save us.
Amen

Learning from our fathers and mothers

Dan 9:4–10; Ps 79; Lk 6:36–38

> *'I pleaded with Yahweh my God and made this con-*
> *fession ...'* (Daniel 9:4)

There are parts of the Book of Daniel that read as if they are modern memoir, written in the first person familiar. 'I, Daniel, was studying the scriptures,' he begins in today's reading. Daniel realizes that a confession had to be made; not a confession for his personal transgressions, but for those of his people, his parents, his nation. 'I turned my face to the Lord God,' he continues, and he did penance. Imagine that—doing penance for the sins of others! I rarely, if ever, do penance for my *own* sins.

God knows that our people, our nations, need prayer and forgiveness! Especially now, in these recent days and years. In his encyclical, *Spe Salvi*, Pope Benedict XVI said: 'We should recall that no man is an island, entire of itself. Our lives are involved with one another, through innumerable interactions they are linked together. No one lives alone. No one sins alone. No one is saved alone. The lives of others continually spill over into mine: for better and for worse. So my prayer for another is not something extraneous to that person, something external, not even after death. In the interconnectedness of Being, my gratitude to the other – my prayer for him – can play a small part in his purification.' (para 48)

The immediate context of the Pope's remarks was to speak about praying for the dead. However, the same ideas hold tremendous potential for praying for those who are alive – and whose actions require confession and penance, whether they realize it or not. Today I will pray for my country, my family, and myself, and I will offer a confession for the wrongs we have done.

Thought for the day
How will you do penance for the sins of your people, your nation, this year?

Prayer
Take our failings, Lord,
as well as our good work in the world,
and sanctify all of it,
for your glory.
Amen

Placing value on something so unheralded

Is 1:10, 16–20; Ps 51; Mt 23:1–12

> *'You have only one Master, and you are all brothers.'*
> (Matthew 23:8)

Jesus shook people up when he began talking about the virtues of humility. A debunker of pride, Jesus saw the worst pride of all in the hearts of religious people. We want people to see our good works. We love to sit in prominent places, have others notice when we are in church or in deep prayer or when we are doing something splendidly spiritual. To be honoured and to honour – those were the religious ways in the time of Jesus.

Times haven't changed much, have they?

'The greatest among you must be your servant,' Christ says in Matthew 23:11. He was only echoing what his followers had heard him say many times before. 'Blessed are the poor in spirit: the kingdom of Heaven is theirs' (Matthew 5:3). Jesus sought to overturn the measure of a person's faith; he called it – surprisingly to the religious people who were listening – simple, meek, poor, child-like. And the kingdom of Heaven – desired by all – he compared to treasure one would hide from others, and to the smallest of seeds, and to yeast, which mysteriously and silently causes the bread to rise.

At those times when I'm feeling the most spiritual, I try and remember that it was the closest friends of Jesus who betrayed him in his final hours. It was the inner circle of our Lord who went to sleep as he was weeping in pain and anticipation in the Garden. And then it was

28

his best friends – the ones who loved him the absolute most – who wandered away as he carried his cross to Calvary, and then denied that they even knew him in the final moments.

I would have been no different!

Thought for the day

Can you identify a sin in your heart, hidden from others, that becomes visible only to you (and to God) at precisely those moments when you feel the most spiritual?

Prayer

Gracious God,
teach us your ways of love and mercy.
Show us the path to forgiving
others, as you have
forgiven us.
Amen

The dumbfounded mother of James and John

Jer 18:18–20; Ps 31; Mt 20:17–28

> *'Anyone who wants to become great among you must
> be your servant'* (Matthew 20:26)

A good mother would ask, wouldn't she? There's no
harm in asking. Consider my sons, she asked our Lord.
Perhaps they are the greatest of your followers, deserv-
ing positions of prominence in your kingdom? (Be sure
to notice, in this story, that these sons of hers – they were
not boys! – James and John, came to Jesus together with
their mother. No wonder the other ten disciples were
'indignant'!)

But the mother of Zebedee's sons must have been
shocked by the teachings she heard from her boys'
Master. Did I hear him correctly, that the humble are
the ones who will be exalted? Doesn't he understand the
value of a good pedigree and hard work? – we can
imagine her thinking.

Presumably, some time went by between the mother's
request (Matthew 20:20–23) and Jesus' explanation to all
of the twelve (vs. 24–28). It seems to have been several
minutes – probably just about as long as it took for
Mother Zebedee to take her leave. Here again, just like
yesterday, we return to see Jesus placing value on
spiritual poverty rather than religious success. In this
anecdote, so easily understood by anyone who has had a
proud mother, we again see how those closest to Christ
seemed unable to 'hear' the radical nature of his teachings. Even disciples like James and John had to unlearn

bad religious and spiritual habits like pride, the desire to perform, and the love of leading.

Jesus instituted a radical form of leadership that was supposed to (but still rarely does) transform people in the spirit of Christ.

Mother Zebedee was dumbfounded, as we surely would have been, as well.

Thought for the day
What sort of leader are you in your work, your family, your church?

Prayer
God,
create in me a clean heart,
and show me how to do your work in humility,
away from the eyes of others.
Amen

The path to blessings

Jer 17:5–10, Ps 1; Lk 16:19–31

> *'Such a person is like a tree by the waterside that thrusts its roots to the stream'* (Jeremiah 17:8)

Jewish midrash (the tradition of telling new stories that help to explain the nuances of the stories of the Bible) makes an intriguing addition to the story of the Exodus from Egypt: As the first Jews approached the Red Sea, with Egypt at their backs and the Promised Land straight ahead, the Sea did not divide in the way that it did for Charlton Heston on the big screen. In fact, the Red Sea did not divide until the very moment that the first man plunged himself into it up to his chin.

The point of the midrash is simple: We are co-creators with God. God does not wish for us to sit back and wait for him to act; we are supposed to be like God as best we can, in our world. And then, if we are busy about God's work, we will be surprised at how miraculous the world can become.

Prophets like Jeremiah tell us over and over again that we will be blessed if we reject evil and keep company with those who do good. It is clear that we have to will to do what is right – 'delight in the law … murmur[ing] God's] law day and night' (Psalm 1:2); it doesn't happen by accident. You cannot usually fall into doing good. And our beautiful Psalm for today adds: If you do this, your life will bear fruit and you will succeed 'like a tree planted near streams' (Psalm 1:3).

Thought for the day

What in your spiritual life needs starting, today? Identify where you have not yet acted, get yourself going, and God will reward you.

Prayer

God of blessings and of love,
show me your strong hand, today
as I recommit myself to staying your course,
honoring your name,
and loving you by loving others.
Amen

The kingdom of God is for the rejected

Gen 37:3–4, 12-13, 17–28; Ps 105; Mt 21:33–43, 45–46

> *'Jacob loved Joseph more than all his other sons...But his brothers ... came to hate him'* (Genesis 37:3–4)

In today's reading from Matthew chapter 21, the wicked tenants kill the landowner's son, the one who was sent by his father. In telling the tale, Jesus says that, as a result, the landowner 'will bring those wretches [who did it] to a wretched end.' He is telling a story that is a metaphor about God the Father and God the Son. Jesus was reject-ed and killed just like that poor landowner's son. He had been sent to do the work of the Father – work that was intended to help those to whom he was sent – and he was hated for it.

The same was true of Joseph, the son of Jacob, as we see in our first reading from Genesis chapter 37. His father favored him, and Joseph flourished, to the great resentment of his brothers. If you are a sibling, the chances are that you have felt, at one time or another, that your mother or father loved one of the others more than they loved you. I am the younger brother and I know that I had such thoughts when growing up.

Each of us has felt rejected at one time or another. Have you ever been loved by someone, and then rejected by that person? Have you offered your love to others, only to have that gift turned away? We have all had some of these experiences. In fact, we spend our lives trying desperately to avoid such feelings, don't we? Well, the Bible shows us again and again that the kingdom of God is for just these sorts of people – each one of us.

And rather than structure our lives so as to avoid caring so as to avoid getting hurt, we are supposed to love in dangerous ways.

Dangerous to ourselves.

Thought for the day
Jesus showed us the way to love, even though our love often goes unreturned. Like Joseph, who loved his brothers even after they despised and almost killed him, we can love dangerously, too.

Prayer
God of love,
forgive my our trespasses,
as I forgive those who trespass against me.
And show me how to love people courageously, today.
Amen

Which son are you?

Mic 7: 14–15, 18–20, Ps 103:1–4, 9–12; Lk 15:1–3, 11–32

> *'Your brother has come, and your father has killed the calf we had been fattening because he has got him back safe and sound.'* (Luke 15:27)

Jesus's parable of the prodigal son is also a parable about the dutiful son. The prodigal son returns and is forgiven his great sins, and then what happens? He is feted! Meanwhile, the dutiful son is left to wonder: Why not me? I've been here, faithfully, all along!

My paternal great-grandmother was born in Italy and several years ago, I travelled back to her small village near Parma. I carried an old photograph that showed my great-great-grandfather. I looked in the phone book and found the address of a distant relative and rang the bell of his apartment building. He was home! Barely speaking each other's languages, this distant cousin invited me up and I quickly realized that he had the very same photograph hanging on his wall!

We visited for several hours, and talked about my great-great-grandfather, Achille. As it turned out, this cousin recounted how his dear mother had often warned him in the sternest of tones: 'Don't grow up to be like Achille!' Apparently, my ancestor had fled the old country for America because he got a girl pregnant and was fleeing the responsibility!

This distant cousin of mine was one of the dutiful sons left behind, as in our reading. He had few great sins and fewer terrific repentances from sin. His life was boring by comparison to Achille. But it is good to be like the dutiful son. 'My life has been happy in doing what God asks of me,' he said that day.

Thought for the day
Who could you fete today, who has been faithful to you and to God?

Prayer
Bless Yahweh, my soul,
As the height of heaven above earth,
so strong is his faithful love for those who fear him.

(Ps. 103:1, 11)

Amen

John Bell

Third Week of Lent

Third Sunday of Lent

Commandments and laws

Ex 20 1–7; Ps 19; 1 Cor 1: 22–25: Jn 2, 13 –25

God spoke all these words. (Exodus 20.1)

Commandments are what God speaks: laws are what humans write. There's a difference.

The first are given out of love to safeguard the future; the second are often codified because of a breach of acceptable behaviour. But they are not the same.

Perhaps rather than talk about 'commandments', we should talk about God's 'gracious words.' For that is what they are. There is nothing in the Ten which is primarily restrictive. Each is meant to liberate.

To have one God, who is above all, freed the early Jews from a culture in which different deities governed different aspects of daily life. In Roman and Greek civilizations such gods had proper names. Today their equivalents have company names or brand names which vie with each other for our attention and assent, and which hold us captive.

To keep the Sabbath holy was intended not to be restrictive but to be life enhancing. It meant that everyone (slaves as well as their owners) was guaranteed a rest. And, by extension, it implied that the earth and its creatures also deserved down-time … something which in our present context seems like paradise.

To refrain from giving false evidence against a neigh-bour not only freed innocent people from the savagery of malicious gossip and tyranny of costly litigation; it also encouraged a respect for people whose opinions or lifestyle might encourage the rumour-mill in advance of the truth of their situation being fully known.

Go through the Ten and look for the liberation implicit in each gracious word. It's a far cry from the legalism which humanity is ever tempted to use in order to ensure the privileges of the elite. This is what so infuriated Jesus when he set the cat among the pigeons in the Temple. The very place where God's graciousness should have been celebrated and enjoyed had instead become a re-stricted environment hedged round by petty legislation and an obsession with things of secondary importance. Jesus would have none of it.

When we think of the Ten Commandments, let us not imagine God like a hanging judge staring in censorship and condemnation on quivering criminals. Let us think more of the most loving of parents who to her or his child gives a well-chosen gift saying, 'Take this. I give it out of love, just for you.'

Thought for the Day
Can I live today both obeying the law, but more keenly keeping the commandments?

Prayer
Gracious God,
thank you that, despite your power,
you do not bully us,
but seek our welfare as if it were your own.
Amen

Favouring without favourites

2 Kings 5:1–15; Ps 42–43; Lk 4: 24–30

> *Only one leper was healed – Naaman, the Syrian.*
> (Luke 4:27)

The cross was not the only attempt made on Jesus' life. The first indirect attempt led to what we call 'The Slaughter of the Innocents.' That was when Herod, fearing that Jesus would become a rival monarch, decreed that all male children of his age should be killed.

The first direct attempt happened within religious precincts – in his home synagogue. The intriguing question is Why? Did he say insulting words to the congregation in the way that a precocious and insensitive young preacher might let his home church 'have it'? No.

Did he divert from the simple exposition of the scriptures into some polemic rant against the forces of political oppression which people seemed inured to? No. Did he spout trendy theology which would upset the guardians of orthodoxy? No again.

All he did was to remind people of their history by taking two instances recorded in the Hebrew Scriptures of how God does not regard those who believe they are 'chosen' as the only people worth saving. So Elijah – in God's name – cares for a non-Jewish widow during a period of famine; and Elisha – again in God's name – enables the curing of a non-Jewish leper. And all this happens despite the prevalence of poor widows and lepers within their own faith communities.

We can read this story as indicative of how God's love

is all embracing, how the barriers which humanity erects have no influence in the way our Maker shows and shares compassion.

And, noting how Jesus occasionally identified in non-Jews (Romans, Samaritans etc) virtues he doesn't see in among his own people, we may be challenged to think about whether we are as generous when it comes to Muslims, Sikhs, Hindus or people of no faith.

Or we may take this story as a challenge to us to ponder whether there are aspects of our own personal, religious or national history which we conveniently forget lest they trouble us. 2007 enabled many especially to see Britain's affluence in the perspective of the slave trade from which our nation greatly profited before its abolition. Was the despised Emily Pankhurst a latter day Elijah, and the equally suspected Gandhi a latter-day Elisha? Time will tell, if only we do not censor history.

Thought for the Day
What in my forgotten past might be intended, by God, for my mending?

Prayer
Enable us, loving God,
not only to see the good in people different from ourselves
but also to see Jesus who is behind all goodness
and brother to every man and woman.
Amen

A forgetful God?

Dn 3:25, 34–43; Ps 25; Mt 18, 21–35

> *Remember, Lord, your tender care and unfailing love.*
> (Psalm 25:6)

Why should God be encouraged to remember? Is it that there are so many things on the divine mind that God cannot focus? Or does God suffer from dementia with short-term memory loss?

It certainly seems an odd thing to say. But this is not an isolated incident. Frequently the psalm writers ask God to remember historical events, vicious enemies or their own parlous states of wellbeing. It seems odd that such a memory note has to be slipped to the one who notes even the death of a sparrow and counts all the hairs on our head.

However, in the context of Psalm 25, the request that God should remember tender care and unfailing love comes after a request that God should forget 'the sins and offences of my youth.'

This is not plea-bargaining before a local magistrate; this is conversation between people who love each other. The writer is, as it were, reviewing his past in the company of his Maker. He is musing over a range of circumstances in which he felt the absence or presence of God. He senses shame for some incidents and finds encouragement in others. The dialogue is like one lover saying to the other, 'Don't remind me of how lousy I was to you. Think of the good times we had together. You were responsible for these.'

It is not that God is absent minded, it is that we have

from time to time to remind ourselves of what God has done and how far we have come by God's guiding.

Sometimes I ask members of a congregation to list all the major changes in the past 50 years. Usually one cynic will comment, 'Oh that won't take long.' But then we begin to list the changes: how women are given equal treatment to men, how children are welcomed, how the language of worship has changed, how rented pews are no longer commonplace, how access is easier for people who are disabled, how we no longer call inhabitants of the southern hemisphere, 'the heathen in their darkness.'

If we went further back we would find greater embarrassments – how British clergy approved of everything from the slave trade to the Highland clearances; how the grief of a miscarriage or still-born child was seldom acknowledged, how churches were sometimes erected by the wealthy as little more than monuments to their own egocentricity.

Think through our pasts – communally and collectively – and there will be several moments when, like the psalm writer, we might want to say to God, 'Don't remember the mistakes of the past, but remember with us the changes which you have enabled for our own good.'

Thought for the Day.
Which blessings will I count before the day grows older?

Prayer
God give us long memories of blessing and short
      memories of hurt.
And, trusting you for what has been,
help us to be aware of the next corner around which
      you wish to nudge us.
Amen.

Wholehearted praise, holistic discipleship

Dt 4: 1,5–9; Ps 147; Mt 5; 17–19

> *God sends his command over the earth and his word*
> *runs swiftly.* (Psalm 147:15)

At first it is national restoration, then it is victim support. From there it moves to astronomy, philosophy, justice, agriculture, meteorology and verbal inspiration, with a passing glance at horse stamina and the lower limbs of athletes.

This could be a description of the contents list of a truncated encyclopaedia, the agenda for a morning news programme or an allusion to the primary concerns of certain government ministers. But it is none of these things.

The diversity of subjects mentioned above are all concerns of God. And Psalm 147, which celebrates the multi-facetted nature of our Creator, pays more than passing mention to each.

Here national security and ecological integrity go hand in hand. Here practical compassion and spiritual wisdom are closely interlinked. Here the praise of God is not divorced from the daily delights and concerns of humanity.

This is what makes our faith so holistic. We cannot corral God and God's word into bland categories of convenience. The Kingdom of Heaven will not be restricted by the fond and often predictable vocabulary which permeates hymns and liturgies. God's creation is diverse and God's redemption is of creation, not simply of the church and related religious matters.

Ironically, it is perhaps the very existence of church buildings, beautiful as they may be, which sometimes restricts our sense of God's adventurous designs. In ancient times, there were no buildings. Worship happened in the open air, and everything done in the open air – from the breastfeeding of babies to preparations against alien invasions – became the stuff of prayer.

Moses, David, Martha and Mary were not depicted as stern but anaemic stained glass stooges, they were thought of as fellow travellers in the journey of faith. Jesus was not the paragon of mildness, he was the sun behind all suns, as dazzling in beauty and energy as the title of 'bridegroom' evokes.

At the beginning of the twenty-first century we do not need more insipid liturgies in honour of a limp deity. We need a healthy planet, a just international economic system, a cessation of violence, a fondness for the earth we inhabit, and a sense of the bigness of God … the kind of subject matter we find in Psalm 147.

Thought for the Day
Is there anything which is unfit to be raised to God in prayer?

Prayer
You are greater than our best imagining,
deeper than our most profound thought of you,
more dynamic than all the energies of earth;
yet you have time for each of us.
Thank you for being a big God who stretches us.
Amen

Living easily with lies

Jer 7:23–28; Ps 95; Lk 11: 14–23

> *Truth has perished; it is heard no more on their lips.*
> (Jeremiah 7:28)

There is a common phrase which all of us say and hear daily, used to preface statements which can be of little or great consequence. It is: 'To tell you the truth …'

In a positive light, this may seem to be a necessary preface to a statement which might at first seem astounding. Hence Jesus, as translated in the Authorised Version of the Bible, sometimes begins a surprising claim by saying, 'Verily, verily I tell you …'

But we are not all or always like Jesus. 'To tell you the truth' could also suggest that the speaker normally tells half truths, but on this occasion it is integrity which prevails. We are right to be cynical, for much of what we hear at a national, let alone a personal level, is a confection of gossip or an avoidance of honesty.

It may have been a chimney sweep who originated the phrase, 'There's no smoke without fire' but it was a politician who popularised the notion of being 'economical with the truth.' And journalists have developed the art of making unrelated innuendos into a jigsaw of conjecture to suit the appetite of a public for whom deceit is more of an amusement than an affront.

It is not for nothing that one of the most proscribed sins in Holy Scripture is that of lying, whether it takes the form of malicious gossip which degrades individuals, or the slandering of other peoples which can lead to racism and war. In order to prove one's self-righteousness, it is very tempting to depict an opponent as defective. But righteousness is its own defence. When it needs to be proved, it deserves to be suspected.

Years ago, when a number of nations had been identified as potential threats to Western security, a Norwegian priest took sabbatical leave to visit the condemned countries. In each of them he recorded mothers singing to their children and eventually published a CD entitled 'Lullabies from the Axis of Evil'. It was a beautiful foil to the demonising intention of that now famous phrase, for it enabled people to recognise that within each of the proscribed nations were people of goodness, love and tenderness.

When Jesus says that 'the truth shall set you free' he is offering a yardstick both in himself and in his Gospel of what it means to live a life of total honesty. By contrast those responsible for his crucifixion had to rely on unfounded gossip. That, along with unfulfilled good intentions, paves the road to hell. The truth as articulated by Jesus is what ensures resurrection.

Thought for the Day
He/she/they are *who* they are, not *what* is said of them.

Prayer
God, my Creator,
since you have seen me in the womb
and know all that is in me,
let no duplicity be on my lips,
or compromise my fidelity.
Amen

The non-obscenity

Hos 14: 2–10; Ps 81; Mk 12: 18–34

Accept our wealth. (Hosea 14:2)

There are two aspects of life which are regularly associated with obscenity, and both are gifts of God.

The first is sex, celebrated for its eroticism in the biblical book variously called The Song of Songs or The Song of Solomon. There is nothing sordid here, nor was there a negative tag to God's initial gendering of male and female. And this precious gift which enhances human living should not have its goodness eclipsed by an obsession with its misuse.

The other matter is equally vilified but, if anything, talked about in even more hushed tones than sex. It is money. It is the commodity to which the adjective 'dirty' is commonly affixed. It is something whose alleged obscenity leads to it to being 'laundered.' Its misuse sometimes requires the wealthy to 'come clean.'

And for many Christians, it is a no-go area. We would rather discuss our sex-life or rehearse our funeral than talk about money. How much we have; whether it is a joy or a burden; how we use or dispose of it … such matters are not often up for public or personal discussion. It is almost as if it were an obscenity, conversation about which would dismay the Almighty.

But God has created a world in which finance is as much of a necessity as culture. And Jesus did not come to hush all conversation about economics – personal or corporate. Quite the opposite. Most of his parables are either about money or food. He befriends people who have money. Simon the Pharisee, Matthew, Zaccheus, Martha and Mary, Lazarus, Joanna and Susanna, Jairus, the Roman Centurion with the sick servant, Nicodemus and many others were wealthy people. He did not chastise them because they could afford to offer him hospitality. He did not return after the resurrection and condemn Joseph of Arimathea for being wealthy enough to offer his grave. He did not turn with revulsion from the person known as 'the rich young ruler'; the Gospel records that 'his heart went out to him.'

However, what can be said consistently from a biblical perspective is that God never views wealth in isolation from poverty. Nor can we, for statistics regularly make us aware that the lot of world's poorest is directly related to the affluence of the world's wealthiest. And Jesus, who recognised the potential in wealth and wealthy people does not simply want us to note the disparity. He wants us to end it.

Thought for the Day
If I were one of the world's poorest, would I believe that God favoured the affluent?

Prayer
Accept our wealth.
Enable us to lay it all on the table before you
so that we may not receive you in the eucharist
while offering only the dross of our devotion.
Amen

Hidden righteousness

Hos 5: 15–6:6; Ps 51; Lk 18: 9–14

> *The other man would not even raise his eyes to heaven.*
> (Luke 18:13)

Jesus' parable of the two men going up to the temple to pray is a work of the imagination. It is highly unlikely that he ever heard a Pharisee loudly advertising his piety so that not only God but other worshippers might hear. And it is equally unlikely that he would have got close enough to hear the mumbled entreaty of the guilt-ridden tax collector.

The parables are not historical reminisces, they are teaching modules. But that in no way diminishes their truth. And in any case God, who knows the secrets of every heart, would be privy to the content of each man's devotion.

What this parable invites us to recognise is that God is not impressed by a catalogue of good deeds done, rituals completed, tithes paid on time, temptations avoided as if such achievements combined to qualify us for a PhD in worthiness. We should be good not out of expectation of reward or fear of punishment. We should be good, act justly, treat others generously, because goodness is intrinsically fulfilling. And if we reflect on those who have touched our lives in transformative ways, they will not be peddlers of self-righteousness, but people for whom kindness is as natural as breathing, and sacrificial kindness a product of love.

The distinctive thing about the tax collector in Jesus'

parable is that he doesn't attempt to compete with the declarations of virtue from the Pharisee, though perhaps he could have. Nor does he scrape the barrel of his distant past to remind God of some long-forgotten instance when his virtue shone through.

No. He is not dependent on himself in the face of his Maker. Rather, he is totally dependent on the grace of God. His prayer, 'Lord, have mercy on me, a sinner' neither catalogues his imperfections or petitions God for a variety of desirable outcomes. But like a child clinging to her mother because she is the guarantor of the child's future, so the tax-collector takes hold of God's promise of forgiveness on which all life depends.

Perhaps that is why we are moved when we hear – in innumerable settings – the tax-collector's prayer as choirs and congregations sing 'Kyrie eleison' (Lord have mercy). There is nothing sophisticated about the text, but it articulates our deep yearning – for forgiveness? Yes. But also for spiritual nourishment, for belonging, for cherishing, for connectedness with that which is the stuff of heaven.

Thought for the Day

Should I make my prayers shorter, but my trust in God greater?

Prayer

Kyrie eleison   (Lord, have mercy)
Christe eleison   (Christ, have mercy)
Kyrie eleison   (Lord, have mercy)

Shirley du Boulay

Fourth Week of Lent

Fourth Sunday of Lent

Courage

1 Sam 16:1, 6–7, 10–13; Ps 23; Eph 5:8–14; Jn 9:1–41

> *'How shall we sing the Lord's song in a strange land?'*
> (Psalm 137, v. 4)

The Jews were in exile, weeping by the waters of Babylon for their home. Their captors asked them to sing the songs of Zion and they could not do it – they hung their harps in the poplar trees and kept their sad silence.

They could not forget Jerusalem but they could not sing Yahweh's songs in a strange land, especially they could not sing to entertain those who had taken them captive. That is one reaction to a tragic situation – keep the songs of your faith precious and tight to your chest. Do not evangelise, do not share – especially with the unsympathetic.

Exile is tragic, yet it was their very exile which forced the Israelites to find new directions; as a result they were renewed.

Christians in the twenty-first century often feel themselves to be a sad minority, struggling to live their faith in a strange land. We are in a minority, living among those who at best do not share our faith, at worst find it wrong, misguided, even pathetic. How do we keep the flame alight in such a time? How do we sing the Lord's

Song when all around us reverberate the sounds of the songs of the great gods of money, possessions, competitiveness and power? How do those who are rejected, persecuted, even imprisoned, keep their voices strong and clear?

Even if we are left to practise our faith, being slighted and mocked is not easy to bear; it takes courage to stand up for a religion that not only takes second place to materialism, but is coming to be overwhelmed by other religions, such as Islam.

But if we can only hold firm. Sing our songs, whether anyone listens or not, whether or not we are in a spiritually strange land. Then maybe we too will find we are led to find new directions. To forge a Christian life that loses nothing of its original truth but is appropriate to our times.

Perhaps we too, lost and out-numbered in our own land, may, like Israel, find renewal.

Thought for the Day

Let us think of those who are, at this moment, suffering for their faith.

Prayer

Give us courage, Lord, to stand by the truth of our faith.
To live your truth as we understand it.
Never to be forced by fear to be silent when the truth
  needs to be declared.
Amen

Gratitude

Is 65: 17–21; Ps 30; Jn 4: 43–54

> *'O Lord my God, I will give thanks unto you for ever.'*
> (Psalm 30, v. 12)

I read recently of a young woman from Lesotho who had been raped, made pregnant and become HIV positive. She then found the virus had passed to the man she loved and wanted to marry and that her two sisters and her mother were also affected. Yet, said someone who met her, she was one of the happiest people she had ever met.

Some years ago I was fortunate enough to meet the wonderful cellist Jacqueline du Pre. She had had to give up her beloved cello because of the ravages of multiple sclerosis. Yet the phrase she used more than any other was, 'I am so lucky. I am so lucky.'

We are taught as children to say Thank you, but gratitude is not just an exercise of good manners, it is an attitude of mind, a great gift and a blessing on both giver and receiver. It is also a quality we can work on and develop simply by remembering to be grateful and, whenever possible, expressing our thanks.The Buddha tells us to be thankful for each day if only because if we didn't learn a lot, at least we learnt a little.

Gratitude can be shown for very small things. I am constantly impressed these days that car drivers seem much more willing to give way when one needs to turn in their path and, when you do the same for them, there is the quick acknowledgement, if just a tiny movement of the hand. I am sad that the 'Thank you letter', once a regular acknowledgement of gifts or hospitality, is becoming a rarity.

Gratitude does not depend on having what we want, it depends on our attitude to what comes our way. We have so much to be grateful for and we need to show it. The aborigines will thank a cabbage before they pick it. We need to show our gratitude to each other, to life itself and, most of all, to the creator, preserver and sustainer of ourselves and of our world.

As the mystic Meister Eckhart said, 'If the only prayer you said in your whole life was "Thank you" it would be enough.'

Thought for the Day

'Gratitude is not only the greatest of virtues, but the parent of all the others.' (Cicero)

Can we express our gratitude to at least two people today?

Prayer

Lord, the source of all we treasure,
let me always show my gratitude to you
and to those who, through you, act kindly towards me.
Amen

Stillness

Ezek 47: 1–9, 12; Ps 46; Jn 5: 1–3, 5–16

'Be still, and know that I am God.' (Psalm 46, v. 10)

I was a terrible fidget as a child – my mother was always telling me to keep still. Even now I find it difficult to keep completely still for long periods and admire so much those unmoving figures one sometimes sees, sitting motionless in meditation. Keeping the body still is hard. It demands self-control. The sole of your foot itches and you long to scratch it; oh what a relief. But minutes later another itch appears on your arm … there is no end to it. There are, however, rewards when one can remain physically still. The body leaves its restlessness, its constant motion, its preoccupation with itself, and sinks into quiet. Muscles untie themselves, pains lessen, breathing steadies.

Stillness of mind is even harder. There are so many thoughts to divert one's attention, each chasing the other out of your mind as another attraction lures you on. The shopping list is replaced by worry about a relationship, looking forward to a social occasion takes its place. They all seem more attractive than the stillness that you are seeking.

We can learn stillness from nature. Sit and watch a tree growing. Even as the branches are blown about, the roots are still. Its stillness is infectious. Animals too have much to teach us. Watch a cat, never making an unnecessary movement.

Do not worry if there is external noise, that need not

disturb your inner silence. It is harder, though, to ignore the inner noise, as the over active mind, 'the monkey mind', leaps from branch to branch and tries to disturb the stillness that you are beginning to scent. As a meditation teacher once said, don't try *not* to think, just show your thoughts the door.

Just be still.

Stillness is the opposite of the frantic acquiring of knowledge and skills, yet answers to problems can be found in its quiet embrace. Out of stillness the right course of action often simply appears. By letting desires go and remaining still and receptive, answers will come and peace becomes a possibility.

And in stillness we have some chance of encountering the peace of God.

Thought for the day
Why not try to sit completely still for ten minutes today?

Prayer
Lord, help us to be still in body, mind and spirit
that in that stillness we may become nearer to you.
Amen

Closeness to God

Is 49: 8–15; Ps 145; Jn 5: 17–30

> *'The Lord is nigh unto all them that call upon him, to all them that call upon him in truth.'*
>
> (Psalm 145, v. 18)

Where is God for you, now, as you read these words? May I hazard a guess? It is quite possible that if you are unhappy, down in the dumps in some way, then he seems to be a long way away. As he was for the Psalmist, when he cried out, 'O God, thou hast cast us off, thou hast scattered us, thou hast been displeased; O turn thyself to us again.'

If, however, you are feeling content, peaceful, loving – then he seems close. As close as the clothes on your body, as close as the skin on your face.

Of course it is possible to come close to God when we are unhappy, but if he joins us in our sadness we are unlikely to remain sad for long. Our real sadness is when we feel God is absent, for then we are split inside ourselves, for we are made to be one with God.

There is a Russian saying that when you're feeling really good, it is as if you were 'tucked into Jesus' shirt.' God is closer than the air we breathe.

If only we could realise that God is with us now and always. He never leaves us; it is we who leave him. As Meister Eckhart said, 'God is at home. It is we who have gone out for a walk.'

The closeness of God is beautifully illustrated by a story of a father trying to teach his son about God. He told his son to put some salt in water and come back the next day. The next morning they looked into the water but could not see the salt, for it had dissolved. So his father said: 'Taste the water from this side. How is it?'

'It is salt.'

'Taste it from the middle. How is it?'

'It is salt.'

'Look for the salt and come again to me.'

The son did so, saying: 'I cannot see the salt. I can only see water.'

His father then said: 'In the same way, O my son, you cannot see the Spirit. But in truth he is here. An invisible and subtle essence is the Spirit of the whole universe. That is Reality. That is Truth.'

We are one with God as the salt is one with the water.

Thought for the day

'Split wood and I am there. Lift up the stone and you will find me there.' (Gospel of Thomas.)

Prayer

Lord let me always remember that we are in you and you are in us.

We cannot be divided.

Amen

Seeking honour

Ex 32: 7–14; Ps 106; Jn 5: 31–47

> *'How can ye believe, which receive honour one of another, and seek not the honour that cometh from God only?'* (John 5, v. 44)

In 2006 a Scottish aid worker, who had been awarded an MBE for her work in the Palestinian refugee camps, returned the award in protest at Tony Blair's handling of the Middle East conflict. She was not the first to make this gesture, nor will she be the last.

We are all thrilled when something we have done is honoured by friends and colleagues – I still remember the delight with which, at the age of about eight, I was awarded a book I did not in the least want but which gave my confidence a boost by recognising some small schoolgirl achievement. It is understandable and for-givable that we should honour each other and rejoice in it. Every year I relish the spontaneous jumping joy of the Wimbledon winner – that high moment in the life of the player has a quality of innocence which never fails to move me.

Yet just as we are not impressed by those seeking honours for their own sake, so we are deeply impressed by those who refuse to play the all too human competitive game. 'Virtue is its own reward' as the old saying has it, with, I feel, a touch of smugness. Truly seeking the honour that comes from God only is even more than that.

The Psalmist is urging us to seek the honour that comes from God only. And that means much more that trying to follow the moral code that Christianity enshrines – that is the relatively easy bit. Sometimes one can recognise this quality in another person - it is radiant and wonderful and you warm your hands on it as at a roaring fire. Their love of God, their total surrender to him, shines from them and you know that that person will have given and given and given, for this path of honouring God only costs not less than everything. It means to accept what life gives you with open hands and, most of all, to love, to love, to love.

Thought for the day
Let us today recognise in another person that quality of seeking God's honour only.

Prayer
Oh Lord
forgive us for seeking the pleasure that comes from
  honours we bestow on each other
and help us to realise that honour can only be found in
  you.
Amen

Hope for the depressed

Wis 2: 1, 12–22; Ps 34; Jn 7: 1–2, 10: 25–30

> 'For they say to themselves, with their misguided rea-
> soning: "Our life is short and dreary,
> nor is there any relief when man's end comes, nor is
> anyone known who can give release from Hades." '
> (Wisdom 2, vv.1, 12–22)

This, surely, is the ultimate text for the depressed. Not
only is our life, apparently, short and sad, but we cannot
even hope to find peace at the last, in the embrace of
death.

Most of us at some time or another experience depression. For some it is a constant and serious illness. Why in
the Bible, of all places, are we given words to sink us
deeper into depression, without even being offered an
escape at the end of our lives?

Perhaps our eyes were drawn to so quickly to the
second line that we missed the first - the assurance that
this is 'misguided reasoning.' Some comfort there, but
the harsh lines still follow. Life is short. Dreary. There is
no relief. Like hammer blows to the depressed spirit.
And from the Book of Wisdom at that. What sort of
Wisdom is this?

Read on and we find the virtuous man is pilloried and
mocked. He claims to have knowledge of God, so will
God rescue him from our common fate? But at last we are
shown the flaw in the argument of those who mock. Just
as we were told that the reasoning of the pessimists was
misguided, now we are assured that the mockers them-

selves are misled, for 'they do not know the hidden things of God.' They have no hope that holiness will be rewarded.

Today's passage leaves us with that thought, but does it help or is it just a cop out? If things are hidden, how can we know and understand them, how can we find hope in them? Read on, and the Book of Wisdom gives real hope:

> The souls of the virtuous are in the hands of God,
> no torment shall every touch them.
> In the eyes of the unwise they did appear to die,
> their going looked like a disaster,
> their leaving us, like annihilation;
> But they are in peace.

Not only comfort – but inspiration. If we try to live good lives we may, in this world or the next, earn that reward.

Thought for the day
However depressed we feel, there is hope, even if it is 'hidden.'

Prayer
Lord when we are bowed down in grief and depression, help us never to forget that we are made in your image and we are in your hands.
Give us your peace.
Amen

The Fourth Saturday in Lent

The enemy within

Jer 11: 18–20; Ps 7; Jn 7: 40–52

> *'O Lord my God, in thee do I put my trust: save me*
> *from all them that persecute me, and deliver me.'*
>
> (Psalm 7, v. 1)

There is nothing quite like extreme danger for throwing
one into the hands of God; for forcing us to realise that,
in certain situations, there is nothing we can do on our
own, that we are totally dependent on God. People in
prison, at the mercy of their captors. People in such
poverty they cannot find the next crust of bread. People
in war, not knowing when the next bullet will strike
them. In such situations our love and dependence grows
stronger and even those who do not consider themselves
believers will call on God to save them, if only because
there is no-one else. God is 'our refuge and strength, a
very present help in trouble.'

But what about the enemies within? What about the
hostile forces within us over which we *can* try to exercise
control? Jealousy, competitiveness, impatience, greed,
pride … We know them, at one level, so well, yet time
and again they win the battle against our peace of mind.
We feel helpless against them.

Perhaps this Lent we might chose one of these negative forces and try to lessen its impact on our lives. We
might take one that does not at first seem so very dread-
ful, like inattentiveness. If we paid more attention to our
friends, when they share their troubles with us; if we
paid more attention to the stories in the newspapers of

terrible suffering endured by innocent men and women. Most of all, if we paid more attention to God, especially in our prayer time. The restless mind loves to wander, but let it spend more time with God, its natural home and only saviour.

Thought for the day
Today I will not just think of God, rather I will try to *be* with God.

Prayer
Oh Lord,
our only protection against the forces that overwhelm us
may our love for you conquer our fear.
Amen

David Adam

Fifth Week of Lent

Fifth Sunday of Lent

Life is for giving: serving brings freedom.

Jer 31:31–34; Ps 51; Heb 5:7–9; Jn 12:20–30

> '*Unless a grain of wheat falls into the earth and dies*
> *...*' (John 12:24)

This passage comes immediately after Jesus' entry into
Jerusalem. His reception by the crowds must have raised
many issues in the minds of his followers.

The Jews dreamt of when they would be free from
captivity: Roman domination would end. They believed
that God would send the Son of Man to lead them to
victory. In the book of Enoch, the Son of Man is seen as a
powerful figure held back at the moment by God. But the
day will come when God will release him on the world.
Nothing will stand against him. Then the Jews will take
control and nations will bow before them. This is a vision
of conquest and of triumphing, no different to the
nations that overpowered them in the past. The Son of
Man would give them the victory. Some looked to Jesus
for such a triumph and his riding into Jerusalem may
have encouraged them – though they failed to see the
donkey, the symbol of peace.

When Jesus spoke of the Son of Man, he spoke of the
giving of life and the pouring out of oneself for others.
The Son of Man does not come seeking the triumph of

power but rather to serve and to give his life as a ransom for many. The glory of the Son of Man was in laying down his life for them. Glory is to be found in serving one another: power is the power of love.

We see conquest as a sign of strength and acquisition as a sign of power. There is still the desire to control others and to lord it over them. We cannot experience the resurrection because we refuse to die to self: new life cannot come because we keep a firm hold on the old. We are afraid of death and so we are unable to live life fully in the pouring out of ourselves in love and service. We feel that we need to control things, our lives, our world and we do not have enough faith to venture, to risk and to say, 'Your will be done'.

Thought for the day

It is in giving that we receive and in dying we rise to eternal life.

Prayer

Dearest Lord, teach me to serve you as you deserve;
To give and not to count the cost,
To fight and not to heed the wounds,
To toil and not to seek for rest,
To labour and not to ask for any reward,
Save that of knowing that I do your will.

(Ignatius Loyola)

Double standards and double dealing

Dan 13:1–9, 15–17, 19–30; Ps 23; Jn 8: 1–11

> *'If there is one of you who has not sinned, let him be the first to throw a stone at her.'* (John 8:7)

Surely there was more than one person involved in this act of adultery! If she was caught in the act how did the man escape? From the outset there are double standards at work: one for the man and another for the woman. The Pharisees were using this woman for their own ends, to trap Jesus.

Such double standards still prevail. Some are privileged and some are not. Such division is of the devil. The devil is often known as Diablo because he throws things apart, is divisive and enjoys double standards. The devil seeks to divide peoples and nations: Christ came that we may be 'one in the Lord.'

There is an awful character in *Wuthering Heights* by Emily Bronte, Joseph the manservant, of whom it is said, he is the 'wearisomest, self-righteous Pharisee that ever ransacked the Bible to rake the promises to himself and fling the curses to his neighbour.' We may smile at this but 'let him who has no sin …'. We often demonise others to glorify ourselves.

Double standards and double dealing are common. We want a good standard of living based on cheap labour from elsewhere. We want to enjoy the pleasures of a developed nation but object to nations that are using resources to catch up to where we are. Multi-nationals make profits by keep the wages of people in poor countries down. We want the blessings and seek not to worry about the curses that we are heaping on others.

The world is still double dealing when only one per cent of women own land and 67 per cent of illiterate people are women. Of the 191 countries in the United Nations only 12 have female leaders. Over large areas of the world women are still treated as inferior to men. If we have a wrong attitude towards others, towards God's creation, we cannot have a right attitude to God or a right relationship with him.

Jesus does not condone sin nor does he condone double standards that make people hypocrites.

Thought for the day
Division is of the devil: Christ brings about at-one- ment.

Prayer
Lord, as we are one in you,
let us show that unity with each other.
Help us to see, that as we deal with the least
so we deal with you.
Amen

The Christ who is ever present

Num 21: 4–9; Ps 102; Jn 8: 21-30

> *'Yes, if you do not believe I am he, you will die in your sins.'* (John 8:24)

The Jews try to escape the challenge of Jesus by mocking him – this is still the defence of many against the call of God. We seek to make light of the most important things of life and get ourselves caught in trivial pursuits. Too often we argue for God when we should present God to people. The Jews suggest they cannot follow Jesus because he will commit suicide, they saw this as the path to hell. Jesus responds by telling them that while he is from above, they are of this world. Their vision and their attitudes are earth bound: they need to set their sights higher, on God and his glory. We tend to live most of our lives without any reference to the mystery and wonder that is always present and we fail to get to the needs of our heart because we skim the surface of life.

We need to accept the great 'I am', the God who is present, who is with us and seeks a living relationship with us. Without this we live well below par, if we can be truly counted as alive at all. 'Sin' in this case means missing the mark. Our aim is too low or we have set our sights wrongly.

The words 'I am' are used in verses 24, 28, 58. On the lowest level it asks the hearers to accept that Jesus is what he says: 'I am what I say.' On the higher level it is a claim to be the Promised One, the Messiah.

In developing our faith we need to meet with the

living God: the God who is. Our God is the God of the past, the future and the present for our God is eternal. Too often we talk about God when we should be talking to him for his is with us now. In the same way we cannot bring God or Christ to anyone for he is with them before we ever arrive, though we can help to make them aware of the present presence in their midst. Learn to see God in others and to share God with others.

Thought for the day

Unless you believe that I am, you will die in your sins.

Prayer

I believe O Christ that you are:
You are present,
You are with us,
You are eternal,
I believe O Christ that you are.
Amen

The service which is perfect freedom

Dan 3:14–20, 24–28, 52–56, Jn 8:31–42

> *If you make my word your home you will indeed be my disciples, you will learn the truth and the truth will make you free.* (John 8:31–32)

These words appear to be addressed to those who say they believe but as yet have not committed themselves. Throughout much of the developed world people say they believe in Jesus Christ but it is a formal statement rather than an act of faith: it is affirming their Christian heritage rather than affirming a relationship with the Living Lord.

People often live off their heritage without contributing to it: they keep traditions and affirm values without living up to them. In this way they are drawing on the deposits that others have placed but not making their own. They are living off the goodness of others and on the mercy of God. Such people are truly bankrupt.

To know the truth is not about knowing in a scientific or intellectual way, it is the knowledge which comes from a relationship with another person. Only through a relationship with Jesus can we come to discover the truth about ourselves and the world. A living relationship with Jesus and what he says will move us into freedom.

So many are afraid to serve him and fail to discover the 'service which is perfect freedom.'

Freedom is a gift from God and comes through our relation to him. Cyril of Jerusalem said of Joseph: 'Joseph was sold to be a bond slave, yet he was free, all radiant in the nobility of his soul'. Once we have received this gift of freedom we are asked to share it, to bring others to it. This will call into question all oppressive regimes, all control over others for our own gain as well as all that seeks to control us. There are plenty of power mad people and control freaks in our world.

Here are some of the freedoms offered to us:

- Freedom from fear – 'You'll never walk alone.' Where we are and wherever life takes us our God is with us.
- Freedom from ourselves – in Christ we are made new.
- Freedom from our sins – from living below par and losing our goal.

Thought for the day
How can we claim to be free if we allow ourselves to be possessed by anything less that the Eternal?

Prayer
Dear Lord,
we pray for the time when all your children shall be free
and the whole earth live to praise your holy name.
Amen

The hide and seek Jesus

Gen 17: 3–9; Ps 105; Jn 8:51–59

> *I know him, and if I were to say: I do not know him, I
> should be a liar, as you are liars yourselves.* (John 8:55)

There is a sense in which Jesus hides himself and wants
us to seek him not only in the depths of the Scriptures
but also within our own lives, in the lives of others and
in the world.

St John's Gospel is like a children's picture book that
you can look at and even enjoy on a surface level, but if
you look more carefully you will discover all sorts of
hidden depths and images. The Gospel can be seen simply as a story about the human Jesus who went about
healing or you can go deeper and discover the hidden
Jesus who is the Messiah, the Christ, and the Son of God.
Many who read the Gospels get no deeper than a story.
John reminds us he has written 'so that you may believe
that Jesus is the Christ, the Son of God, and that believing
you may have life through his name'(John 20:31). The
Scriptures are there for us find the way to Jesus and to
meet with him.

Today's Gospel is full of hidden mystery and wonder
that bursts out:

'Whoever keeps my word will never see death'

'You say "He is our God" although you do not know
him. But I know him'

'Before Abraham ever was, I am'

Here is a promise of eternal life.

Here is a challenge to our awareness and personal

relationship with God the Father. We are to get to know him.

There is an amazing depth in the statement 'before Abraham was I am.' Some have argued that Jesus is only claiming to exist as he stands before the Jews and that there is no explicit linking of himself with the Divine Name as revealed to Moses (Exodus 3:14). Maybe that is so but it is also true there are hidden depths here. St John wants us to look for what is implicit. Can you see the hidden Jesus? Hidden behind words waiting to be revealed is the 'I AM', Eternal One who is ever present and waiting to be found in every encounter and in the cry of the poor and the helpless.

Thought for the day

Lord, I do seek your face; do not hide your face from me. (Psalm 27:9)

Prayer

Lord Christ, eternally present,
open our eyes to see you in all whom we meet
open our hearts to your love
and help us to know you as our Saviour and our God.
Amen

Do not take God's name in vain

Jer 20: 10–13; Ps 18; Jn 10: 31–42

> *'If I am not doing my Father's work, there is no need to believe me.'* (John 10:37)

In January 2008 the UK Parliament considered abolishing the 'Blasphemy Law'. This was because it was limited to the Christian faith. One MP rightly asked, 'God does not need protecting?'

But this is to miss the mark, for though God does not need protecting, people and all of his creation does – from all who will deal contemptuously and without reverence towards them.

It would have been good for the MPs to look at blasphemy in its wider meaning, which means 'to injure one's reputation'. It is concerned with irreverence towards any person or thing, and there is much of this about in our world. It is the opposite of goodness for it shows lack of care or respect for what is around us.

In relation to God, blasphemy is to misuse 'his name' which in fact means his presence and his power. In the wider sense, it is blasphemy to distort or disfigure God's image in us, for it shows disrespect for the Creator. It is blasphemy to destroy creatures and land areas for our own gain for it shows a lack of respect towards the life around us. It is blasphemy to treat any individual badly.

Our attitude to the world and to creation reflects our attitude not only to life but towards God the creator and the giver of life. If we are in a wrong relationship with the world or with each other we cannot be in a right relationship with God.

Christ counters the charge of blasphemy by telling of the good he has done. He has spent his life healing, caring for the sick, feeding the hungry. Which of these cause you to stone me?

Thought for the day

This is blasphemy: to treat any of God's creation with contempt or lack of reverence.

Prayer

Lord, may we show our reverence to you
in the way we deal with the world and with each other.
Let us not take anything or anyone for granted
but give all of your creation the respect that is due.
Amen

The One who dies for the people

Ezek 37:21–28; Jer 31:10–13; Jn 11: 45–56

> *'You fail to see it is better for one man to die for the people, than for the whole nation to be destroyed.'*
>
> (John 11:49)

We see the anxiety that the popularity of Jesus causes among the church leaders. There is fear that a popular uprising could threaten the 'establishment'. Caiaphas and the Sadducees want to keep things as they are, to maintain their privileged position and not have anyone rock the boat. If the Jews caused any 'civil disobedience' Rome would bring all its might down upon them. Later, the destruction of Jerusalem in 70 AD when the Temple was destroyed and a plough drawn across its courtyards is proof that they had good cause to worry.

The Jews believed that the High Priest spoke for God. This ideal of the Church knowing God's will has often been made a mockery of in history. The Church is human with all the failings of humans and needs salvation as much as the individual. Though now looking back the deeper meaning of his words are true.

Caiaphas meant that Jesus should be sacrificed for the nation. It is amazing how often 'extermination' is couched in terms that make it sound as if it was for people's welfare. Often such an act is put forward by the powerful or those who want to keep the status quo. It is put forward by the arrogant that are sure they are better than others, or who are really insecure and feel their positions challenged. Once a course of extermination has started, it tends to grow. They would plot to kill Lazarus also and later the disciples.

People are still removed from their homes, their land and even life itself to suit the 'powers that are in control'. Like the Christ was, they are forced out of our cities – or at least the 'better' parts of our cities – and off their land for the benefit of others.

Jesus went in to hiding. Can you find the hidden Jesus in the words 'it is better for one man to die for the people'? The Jesus who is the 'Lamb of God' (John 1:36): the true Passover Lamb who takes away the sins of the world: Jesus willingly gives his life as a ransom for many (Matthew 20:28).

Thought for the day

Jesus is often found among the scorned and rejected, among those edged out of society and life.

Prayer

Lord Jesus, Lamb of God,
May we see your presence in the oppressed,
in the scorned and rejected
and know that you are
their Saviour and ours.
Amen

Frances Young

Holy Week and Easter Sunday

Passion (Palm) Sunday

Forsaken

Is 50:4-7; Ps 22; Ph 2:6-11; Mk 14:1-15:47

> *'At three o'clock Jesus cried out with a loud voice,*
> *"Eloi, Eloi, lema sabachthani?" which means, "My*
> *God, my God, why have you forsaken me?"'*
>
> (Mark 15:34)

The Japanese novelist, Shusaku Endo, tells the story of a
very ordinary Samurai sent by his Emperor with a
delegation to Europe in 1613. *The Samurai* is a brilliant
evocation of culture shock. Above all the Samurai's
Japanese values are challenged by the honour given to
the 'naked figure of an emaciated man ... carved on the
crucifix'. 'The Samurai gazed at this man, whose arms
were outstretched, and whose head drooped lifelessly.
He could not understand why [the foreigners] called
such a man "Lord".'

The novel tells how his party accepted baptism as a
way of furthering the embassy, and so when years later
they got back to Japan and policy there had changed, he
had another shock. He found himself not received with
honour, and eventually persecuted as a Christian. What
he had never understood he began to appreciate, as he
came across a piece of paper given to him on the journey:

'He is always beside us.

He listens to our agony and our grief.

He weeps with us.

And He says to us,

"Blessed are they who weep in this life, for in the kingdom of heaven they shall smile."'

The Samurai died as a Christian martyr.

The story Mark tells is of one who is progressively forsaken: Judas betrays him, Peter denies him; the disciples all forsook him and fled. The people, who had shouted, 'Hosanna', seeing the way the wind was blowing, now cried 'Crucify him'. The soldiers mock him. Hanging on the cross, he is subjected to taunts – where are all his fine promises now? Not only is he mocked by the religious leaders who have successfully got rid of a trouble-maker, but even by his fellow-criminals. Finally, he knows himself forsaken by God.

Here is the culture shock: God's presence is to be found among those who are utterly forsaken.

Thought for the day

'The SS hanged two Jewish men and a youth in front of the whole camp ... [T]he death throes of the youth lasted for half an hour. As the youth still hung in torment in the noose after a long time, I heard the man call again, "Where is God now?" And I heard a voice inside myself answer: "Where is he? He is here. He is hanging there on the gallows ...". (Elie Wiesel, Night)

Prayer

We turn to you, that we may be forgiven
For crucifying Christ on earth again ... (Fred Kaan)

Monday of Holy Week

Generosity

Is 42.1–7; Ps 27; Jn 12.1–11

> *Mary took a pound of costly perfume … The house was*
> *filled with the fragrance of the perfume.* (John 12.3)

John Wesley told his followers to 'earn as much as you
can, save as much as you can, and give as much as
you can'. In Judaism, Christianity and Islam, almsgiving
has always been an important religious duty. The prob-
lem is that even Judas recognises this! We ought not to
waste things; we ought to give to the poor.

Charles Dickens in his novel, *Bleak House*, creates a
wonderful caricature of a Victorian do-gooder – Mrs
Pardiggle. She was one of 'the ladies who were most
distinguished for … rapacious benevolence' and
belonged to that class of 'charitable people' who 'did a
little and made a great deal of noise', not those who 'did
a great deal and made no noise all'. We are entertained
by a description of how she organised the charitable
giving of her entire family, five sons and a husband,
whether willing or not. We are then taken on one of her
visits to the poor, 'Mrs Pardiggle, leading the way with a
great show of determination, and talking with much
volubility about the untidy habits of the people …' The
family, trapped in dirt and poverty, cringe before her
moral onslaught. There is no compassion, understanding
or friendliness. She patronisingly does her duty.

I shall never forget the administrator of a day centre
for old people, run on church premises with volunteers
from the congregation, commenting that these volun-

teers were 'buying their ticket to heaven'. It is all too easy for do-gooders to be really concerned deep down with their own self-image as 'a good Christian' rather than to be really committed to persons they are seeking to help.

Duty tends to end in compassion fatigue or guilt. The rich salve their guilty consciences by giving to charities at arms' length. A student once spoke of feeling so guilty about sitting down to a good meal when so many in the world are hungry he couldn't say grace. Guilt cripples; guilt precludes gratitude, because guilt is primarily self-interested.

True generosity is an opening of the heart to others, like Mary's spontaneous act of love to Jesus.

Thought for the day

Let holy charity
Mine outward vesture be,
And lowliness become mine inner clothing
                    (Bianco da Siena, tr. R. F. Littledale)

Prayer

Give me the grace, Lord, to receive your bounty with
    gratitude
and pour it forth generously with compassion.
Amen

Tuesday of Holy Week

Control or Trust

Is 49:1–6; Ps 71; Jn 13:21–33, 36–38

> *For you, O Lord, are my hope, my trust, O Lord, from my youth.* (Psalm 71.5)

Peter is sure he's ready to lay down his life for Jesus, but ironically it will be the other way round; and Jesus knows that Peter's fear will force him to lose control – he will deny his master, and then feel deeply ashamed of his failure.

Judas, on the other hand, takes control; and Jesus knows what he will do to precipitate events. 'Do quickly what you are going to do,' he says. Many have tried to understand Judas' motives. Leonid Andreyev, a Russian writer of the early twentieth century, was fascinated by the insoluble paradoxes of the human spirit, and wrote an account of Judas as an intriguing enigma. Greed can hardly be the full explanation when he sold Jesus for such a trifling sum. Andreyev conjures up a picture of a split-personality, a misfit and a trickster, who needs to impress, to get credit and recognition, an intelligent and street-wise character who despises the other disciples, yet is jealous of them – why does Jesus not love him as he loves the others? It is with 'tormented love and heartache' that he kisses Jesus in the Garden. He betrays him out of fanatical devotion, in order to get him to reveal himself to the world. When no miracle happens but events follow their inevitable course, Judas goes through his own agony, mysteriously twinned with Jesus in carrying this burden. Judas tried to take control – to shape things his way.

The passion-story can be read and re-read in so many ways, yet always seems to mirror aspects of our human reality. Over the centuries great literature has engaged with tragedy – with the ways in which human beings try to be like gods, to take control of events only to find they are caught up in things beyond their control; or try to assert what is right in moral conflicts which turn out to be irresolvable; or try to use their strengths to change the world for good, only to find that those good intentions reap the whirlwind.

In the midst of it all Jesus silently lets go control, trusting and hoping.

Thought for the day

Trying to have everything under control, while losing control of ourselves – perhaps this sort of thing (rather than pride, lust, envy, gluttony, anger, etc.) is what shows up the way we fall short of the glory of God.

Prayer

Lead me from death to life, from falsehood to truth;
lead me from despair to hope, from fear to trust;
lead me from hate to love, from war to peace.
Let peace fill our heart, our world, our universe …
Amen

Costing and Pricing

Is 50.4–9; Ps 69; Mt 26:14–25

> *For the Lord hears the needy, and does not despise his*
> *own that are in bonds.* (Psalm 69.33)

In Trollope's novel, *The Way We Live Now*, Melmotte is described as 'the great French swindler who has come over here and who is buying his way into society'. Rumour has it that 'he amasses his money not by honest trade, but by unknown tricks – as does a card-sharper'. He is a 'surfeited sponge of speculation', a 'crammed commercial cormorant". He 'holds the world of commerce in his right-hand'; 'such a man rises above honesty' – 'such greatness is incompatible with small scruples'. 'This man with a scratch of his pen can send out or call in millions of dollars.' 'Wealth is power', and 'power is good'; 'the more a man has of wealth, the greater and the stronger and the nobler he can be'. And almost everyone else in the book gets sucked in because 'it's always important to have a lot of money'.

Not so long ago the BBC broadcast a serial dramatisation of this novel, just over a century after its original publication. Viewers recognised the 'whole jerry-built society of scheming women, money-grubbing aristocrats and blatant millionaires' (Michael Sadlier) as the world they read about in the press of their own time. Today we can see how Trollope's description of speculation in shares in a spoof railway company mirrors the unreality of the financial trading that built up the credit crunch. We too live in a world where everything has its price, where costing is the only measure of value, where love is corrupted into a business transaction.

The price was 30 pieces of silver – in Andreyev's novel Judas is dismayed at the cheap rate put on the life of the one he loved. Maybe Judas didn't do it for the money, but Jesus identified with those betrayed by systems which encourage speculation and greed.

The price was 30 pieces of silver – Jesus' life was cheap, like the lives of those the financial world ignores and exploits. Victims have no redress, as livelihoods are lost, homes repossessed, food priced out of reach, and they are left powerless. Fairness goes out of the window – that is the great betrayal.

Thought for the day

Do justly, love mercy, walk humbly with your God.

(Micah 6.8)

Prayer

Dearest Lord, teach me to be generous ...
To give and not to count the cost,
To toil and not to seek for rest,
To labour and not to seek reward,
Save that of knowing that I do thy will.

(St. Ignatius Loyola)

Foot-washing in community

Ex 12:1–8, 11–14; Ps 116; I Co 11:23–26; Jn 13:1–15

> *Peter said to him, 'You will never wash my feet'.*
>
> (John 13:8)

After returning from a period of ministry in the Honduras, a former student of mine (Michael Austin) wrote a novel called *Searching for Mother*. It tells how a British teacher working in Latin America finds a parcel thrust into her arms in the central square of the capital city, and inside is a baby.

Against all advice, she decides to track down the mother. The journey takes her into the poor shanty-towns around the city, then out into the war-torn countryside. A clandestine two-day hike into the mountains with a boy-guide brings her to a hidden village. The authorities think they are freedom-fighters, *communistas*; but she discovers that their centuries-long struggle is for their identity, their traditions, their community, in the face of colonialist oppression.

She finally wins acceptance among them when the village is attacked, when she herself loses everything she possesses and is raped by American soldiers. Admitted to this community of suffering, she is given the information she needs to find the mother. Back in the capital she tracks down the baby's origins, but already the mother has disappeared. She commits herself to the baby's future, only to find that meanwhile it has died of measles in the orphanage where it had been left. Finally she discovers the rape has left her pregnant. This new life she dedicates to the life of the Tribe that has accepted her.

The book is absolutely realistic about the seeming hopelessness of making a difference. Yet the heroine of the tale is profoundly changed by the experience of community, a deprived community surviving against all the odds, a community able to mourn and celebrate, a community able to share and care. The story is punctuated with moving moments of tender washing – washing the baby, being washed in her trauma by the Indian women.

Jesus tried to show a protesting Peter that communion requires an end to status, and an ability to receive the service of others. By making foot-washing a kind of sacrament, the L'Arche communities express the deep importance of mutual relationships between those requiring care and those who are carers.

Thought for the day
Admiration is not love. Admirable people do not need us. Love implies proximity, mutuality. When people love, they need each other and are vulnerable one to another.

(Jean Vanier)

Prayer
Lord, help me to climb down and let you wash my feet;
then I shall be ready for receiving and giving in community,
for caring and sharing with others.
Amen

The Hour of Glory

Is 52:13—53.12; Ps 31; Heb 4:14–16; Jn 18:1—19:42

> *There they crucified him, and with him two others, one*
> *on either side, with Jesus between them ... He said, 'It*
> *is finished'. Then he bowed his head and gave up his*
> *spirit* (John 19:18, 30)

'For all the torment of your past and future years, my
mama. For all the anguish this picture of pain will cause
you. For the unspeakable mystery that brings good
fathers and sons into the world and lets a mother watch
them tear at each other's throats. For the Master of the
Universe, whose suffering world I do not comprehend.
For dreams of horror, for nights of waiting, for memories
of death, for the love I have for you, for all these things I
remember, and for all the things I should remember but
have forgotten, for all these I created this painting – an
observant Jew working on a crucifixion because there
was no aesthetic mould in his own tradition into which
he could pour a painting of ultimate anguish and
torment.'

Chaim Potok's novel, *My Name is Asher Lev*, reaches a
place of deep hurt and conflict. The boy had had a
compulsion to draw and paint which had caused enough
trouble at home and at school: 'Jews don't draw and
paint'. But as an established artist he finds himself driven
to an act of apostasy – painting his mother against a
window in such a way that it is clearly in the traditions
of Christian depiction of the passion.

This novel forces the reader to see the cross in unexpected ways. We are, of course, reminded of the ultimate torment and sufferings of Jews in the twentieth century; and that Jesus was a Jew. But above all the novel takes us to the depths of personal anguish, of conflicts of loyalty, of the pain of love, and offers the passion as a universal expression of humanity's hurt.

John's Gospel tells a story of light entering darkness, and the hour of deepest darkness is paradoxically the hour of glory. The mystery of pain and suffering is the place where God is met, and there is transfiguration.

But this is not just comfort for believers. Jesus died as an apostate. Jesus died with outsiders. Jesus was caught up in the expediencies forced on a country occupied by foreign oppressors. He exposes and bears the perennial violence of humankind.

Thought for the day

'Reconciliation is no easy option ... After all, it did cost God the death of his Son to effect reconciliation; the cross of Jesus was to expose the sinfulness of sin when he took on the powers of evil and routed them comprehensively. No, just as there can be no cheap grace so there can be no cheap reconciliation, because we cannot cry, "peace, peace" where there is no peace.' (Desmond Tutu)

Prayer

Lord, we stand at the foot of the cross, and see what it takes.
But still we beg you to turn our violence into peace,
our darkness into light,
our anguish into joy.
Amen

The Sacrament of the Present Moment

Rom 6:3-11; Ps 117; Mk 16:1–7

> *Therefore we have been buried with him by baptism into death, so that, just as Christ was raised from the dead by the glory of the Father, so we too might walk in newness of life.* (Romans 6:4)

Two themes are associated with Holy Saturday – one is the notion of living 'between the times', of waiting for fulfilment; the other is baptism, as people 'die and rise with Christ' in the Easter vigil.

The novel *Gilead* by Marilynne Robinson takes us into deeper appreciation of both. It is a delicate portrayal, through his own fictional voice, of an old minister in a one-horse town in Iowa, and a celebration of ordinary goodness in the everyday here and now. Yet because the 'writer' has a heart condition his reflections go beyond the present in a kind of waiting and anticipation: 'This morning I have been trying to think about heaven, but without much success.' He doesn't know why he should 'expect to have any idea of heaven', as he couldn't have imagined this world if he had not 'spent almost eight decades walking around in it'. He can't believe that 'when we have all been changed and put on incorrupt-ibility, we will forget our fantastic condition of mortality and impermanence, the great bright dream of pro-creat-ing and perishing that meant the whole world to us.' He thinks that 'in eternity ... all that passed here will be the epic of the universe, the ballad they sing in the streets'. 'I can't believe we will forget our sorrows altogether. That would mean forgetting we had lived, humanly speaking. Sorrow seems to me to be a great part of the substance of human life.'

And looking back over a lifetime of ministry he ponders blessing and baptism: 'Water was made primarily for blessing, and only secondarily for growing vegetables or doing the washing.' 'Baptism doesn't enhance sacredness but it acknowledges it, and there is power in that. I have felt it pass through me, so to speak. The sensation is of really knowing a creature, I mean really feeling its mysterious life and your own mysterious life at the same time.'

This slow-moving, reflective novel has a surprising dénouement which will not be revealed here – perhaps that too is true to Holy Saturday. The unexpected is just around the corner: Christ is risen. He is risen indeed. Alleluia.

Thought for the day

'Faith is the light of time, it alone recognizes truth without seeing it, touches what it cannot feel, looks upon this world as though it did not exist, sees what is not apparent. It is the key to celestial treasures, the key to unfathomable mystery and knowledge of God.'

(Jean Pierre de Caussade, *The Sacrament of the Present Moment*)

Prayer

Open my eyes, Lord,
to the sacredness of the ordinary;
and open my heart to the sacredness of every human
    creature.
Amen

Astonishment

Acts 10:34, 37–43; Ps 117; Col 3:1–4; Jn 20:1–9

> *'When Christ who is your life is revealed, then you also*
> *will be revealed with him in glory.'* (Colossians 3:4)

Ever since I first read Ben Okri's *Astonishing the Gods*, I've said, 'I don't understand, I must read it again.' One thing it seems to say is, You're not meant to understand: 'When you make sense of something, it tends to disappear. It's only mystery which keeps things alive.' Another thing it suggests is that happiness is not the point: 'We are masters of the art of transcendence. We are masters of suffering.'

Ben Okri's pilgrim is a nameless man, born invisible, who finds himself invisible in the history books, standing surely for the countless millions of the forgotten. Yet it is as he loses his identity and sees things as they are that he is filled to bursting with knowledge and joy. At the end he looks in a mirror and cannot see himself. 'It seems odd and beautiful that he who left home in search of the secret of visibility should have found a higher invisibility, the invisibility of the blessed.'

In that quest, he finds himself in many strange, upside-down places. 'He marvelled at the people who had risen, as if from a millennial sleep … [and] the new civilisation they built … It was the fruit of what they had learned during those long years of suffering and oblivion … They had constructed palaces of wisdom, libraries of the infinite, cathedrals of joy, courts of divine laws, streets of bliss … They had created an educational system in which the most ordinary goal was living the fullest life, in which creativity in all spheres of endeavour was the basic alphabet ...' The dream of the invisibles is to create the first universal civilisation of justice and love.

This beautiful yet enigmatic book conjures up a world both like and unlike our reality, even our dreams. Resurrection encompasses similar paradoxes: Jesus returns to bodily life, yet is not constrained by the usual physical limits. It is new creation, his and ours, like and unlike the life we know. And because he lives, we have a foretaste of this strange new world where the invisibles make a full contribution.

Thought for the day

'Mister God is different. You see, Fynn, people can only love outside and can only kiss outside, but Mister God can love you right inside, and Mister God can kiss you right inside, so it's different. Mister God ain't like us; we are a little bit like Mister God, but not much yet.'

(from *Mister God This is Anna* by Fynn)

Prayer

Death has been swallowed up in victory.
Thanks be to God, who gives us the victory through our
    Lord Jesus Christ.
Amen

Books mentioned in Frances Young's reflections:

Shusaku Endo, *The Samurai*, Penguin Books 1983

Charles Dickens, *Bleak House*, Oxford Classics

Leonid Andreyev, *Judas Iscariot and other stories*, ET London: John Westhouse 1947

Anthony Trollope, *The Way We Live Now*, Oxford Classics

Michael J. Austin, *Searching for Mother*, Palaver Publications 1991

Jean Vanier, *Drawn into the Mystery of Jesus through the Gospel of John*, DLT 2004

Chaim Potok, *My Name is Asher Lev*, Penguin Books 1974

Desmond Tutu, *Hope and Suffering*, Collins: Fount 1984

Marilynne Robinson, *Gilead*, Virago 2004

Jean-Pierre de Caussade, *The Sacrament of the Present Moment*, ET Collins: Fount 1981

Ben Okri, *Astonishing the Gods*, Phoenix 1995

Fynn, *Mister God This is Anna*, Collins: Fountain 1977

CAFOD is the Catholic Agency for Overseas Development. It is the official overseas development and relief agency of the Catholic Church in England and Wales. CAFOD has been fighting poverty in developing countries since 1962.

CAFOD believes that all human beings have a right to dignity and respect, and that the world's resources are a gift to be shared equally by all men and women, whatever their race, nationality or religion.

CAFOD is a member of the Caritas International Federation, a worldwide network of Catholic relief and development organisations.

CAFOD raises funds from the Catholic community in England and Wales, the UK government and the general public so that it can:

- promote long-term development, helping people in need to bring about change for themselves through development and relief work.
- respond to emergencies, providing immediate help for people affected by conflict or natural disasters.
- identify the causes of poverty and raise public awareness of them, encouraging supporters and the public to challenge the structures, policies and attitudes that reinforce inequality.
- speak out on behalf of poor communities, explaining the underlying causes of poverty and challenging governments and international bodies to adopt policies that promote equality and justice.

- promote human development and social justice in witness to Christian faith and gospel values.

Enacting Gospel values

CAFOD's work is one of the ways in which the Church expresses and enacts its belief in human dignity and social justice.

It is inspired by Scripture ('to bring good news to the poor,' Luke 4:18), by Catholic Social Teaching and by the experiences and hopes of the poor, marginalised and often oppressed communities it supports.

It works to enact Gospel values – within and beyond the Church – including:

- concern for our neighbours and the wellbeing of future generations
- serving the common good to enable everyone to develop equally
- fighting for social justice and ensuring everyone's basic needs are met
- acting on the basis of need, not greed, and acting in solidarity with those living in poverty
- promoting the values of human dignity, community, stewardship and the integrity of creation.

CAFOD puts into practice the solidarity and communion for which the Church stands, and strives for a world built on interdependence, mutuality and sharing, where exclusion, exploitation and greed do not exist.

Website: www.cafod.org.uk

In 1945, the British and Irish churches created Christian Aid to put faith into action amid the ruins of a horrific war. Sixty years on, we work with church partners, the ecumenical family and sister agencies as well as with alliances of other faiths and secular groups which share our passionate determination to end poverty.

Christian Aid works wherever the need is greatest – irrespective of religion or race.

Because we believe in strengthening people to find their own solutions to the problems they face, we support local organisations, which are best placed to understand local needs. We also give help on the ground through 16 overseas offices.

Christian Aid Week each year is the largest house-to-house collection in the UK, with the involvement of over 300,000 volunteers and 20,000 local churches and committees.

We strive for a new world transformed by an end to poverty and we campaign to change the rules that keep people poor.

Our values

The essential purpose of Christian Aid is to expose the scandal of poverty, to help in practical ways to root it out from the world, and to challenge and change the systems which favour the rich and powerful over the poor and marginalised.

Put life first

We believe that all people are created equal, with inherent dignity and infinite worth. Individual human needs must always come first, ahead of dogma, ideology or political necessity. We know that each one of us, in all our diversity and varied talents, can make a real difference in the battle to end poverty and injustice.

Struggle for justice

Poverty is a condition created by an unjust society, denying people access to, and control over, the resources they need to live a full life.

So we take the side of poor and marginalised people as they struggle to realise their civil, political, economic, social and cultural rights.

We believe in the just and sustainable use of the earth and its resources, so that the greed of one generation will not create poverty for the next.

Speak out courageously

We have a duty to speak out and act with conviction to challenge and change the systems that create poverty.

Christian Aid always remains independent of governments and other powerful institutions. We work to educate and mobilise people from all kinds of backgrounds to build a global movement which can change the course of history.

Test everything against experience

We know that poor people are the true experts on the nature of poverty, and our work is shaped by their voices and concerns.

In a spirit of humility, we try to learn from our own mistakes and from the experience of those we work alongside, to improve the impact of our work.

We know that lasting solutions can never be imposed on communities from the outside.

Work together with others
All our work is based on the spirit of cooperation and partnership. We help to build a world free from poverty through inter-faith and intercommunity dialogue and cooperation.

We nurture the talents, commitment and energy of all our supporters, volunteers and staff. Together we uphold a commitment to honesty, mutual respect, accountability and diversity.

Towards a new earth

For Christian Aid this is a time to act upon our dream of a new earth on which we all stand equally, to renew our faith and hope, to reaffirm our commitment to the world's poorest communities, and to promote the dignity and rights of people throughout the world.

Website: www.christian-aid.org.uk